Leaves of Light

Poems by Charles Michael Burack

apocryphile press
BERKELEY, CA

Apocryphile Press
1700 Shattuck Ave #81
Berkeley, CA 94709
www.apocryphile.org

The author wishes to gratefully acknowledge the journal *Sufism: An Inquiry*, which published an earlier version of the poem "I Am." In 2012 the poem won first prize in the international Songs of the Soul Poetry Contest.

To My Beloved

Contents

Leaves of Light

ONE

In the beginnings
I am
and in the endings
I am
every finish but a pause
every start but a push
or pull
of infinite pulsations
of endless cyclings and recyclings
birthings and buryings
bloomings and bustings

All I see is I
                    I
is all I see

ALL
always all

Always EACH
always all

Each a part
            a portal
a pris m

Enter a
leaf you are
there Enter a root
you are here
Branch trunk
fruit

                    tree
                    of
                    l i f e

                              Earth is sun's dark
                              condensed rays

                              Sun is earth's light
                              loosened dust

Waves dis sol ve
            into p a r t i c l e s

P a r t i c l e s
            da
          n   ce
              into waves

                    The curve of surf
                              slides ahead
                          of surge
                    and back of
                    sink

                    Who leads?
                        who follows?
                                who?

                    Pick a piece
                    a portion a
                    point
                    and follow it
                    through
                    all the way
                    through
                    til you

                                    return
                              to that place
                              having been
                              everywhere
                                    and
                                 nowhere

Infinite s
        t
          e
            p
              s
                 from ev
                         er
                       y
                        HERE
                            to
                               ev
                                  er

                                           y

                        THERE

                              An
         i   n   f   i   n   i   t   y
                           of infinite-
                              simally
                           small points
                             in every
                             infinite-
                              simally
                               small
                                po
                                in
                                t

                                          Every
                                         vacuum
                                              a
                                          womb
                                             of
                                          being

I am the mother and the baby
and the flow of joy between
I am the mammaries and the milk
and the mouth that sucks blind

                    I am the soldier and the gun
                        and the corpse at his feet
                    I am the black earth crimsoned
                            and the dull gleam
                            in the unliving eye
                    I am the general who gave
                            the command
                        and the wife who weeps
                    when the messenger arrives

                              The trees are my thick hairs
                            the mountains muscled bone
                                  the seas fragrant sweat
                            the winds my living breath

                    I love the fly as well
                        as the fawn
                        the soil as well
                        as the sun
                        the ladder equal
                        to the sickle
                        the mole as much
                        as the man

I pulse
    like a liquid
        snake
   through the veins
  of
a leaf
  and redden
      the rose
    in
  spring

Where hands held hands
I was what I was
Where hearts meet hearts
I am what I am
Where lips will touch lips
I will be what I will be

In the pause before the pulse

In the stillness after the leap

In the potential between the acts

I reign in silence

Can you see
an apple without seeing
the branch the sun the dirt the ants
the spring rain the clouds the nearby lake
the distant sea the farmer the trucker the truck
the steel plant the rubber plantation
the market
place?

I
burn and burn
consuming myself
spreading out my wealth
that all may be
light

Everyone
a ray
rooted
in my burning
heart

Everyone
a root
arrayed
with my fire

My heart
a bright home
an incandescent loam

All am I
All ah All
Allah All

Elo-him
Elo-her
Elo-all
El-o-all
El-Om-all

OM
am
I

ShalOM
I
shall
be

Shantih
Shantih
Shantih

OPEN TO YOU

In prayer and
meditation
I keep hearing
I am to open
to your
presence
wisdom
and love
in all things
at all times
and not to walk
a single
narrow
path

THE DIVINE MARRIAGE

Let us walk together, my beloved,
toward God, with God, in God,
deeper and deeper into Unity,

Each of us a guide, a witness,
a friend and fellow traveler,
a mate and muse on the path of Love.

Let us surrender to the Presence
in each other and bow heads
and anoint toes with kisses and tears.

Let us guard the Pearl of our souls
and drink deep and long the Life
ever flowing from our inmost Heart,

Both of us Beloved's adoring
servants, ecstatic with boundless
service, dancing wildly into night
intoxicated on wine of Eternity
until we collapse in twined arms
and sleep the deep peace of Bliss.

O come, my beloved, come come
soon for the hour is late
and our hearts open and ripe
to drown as one in One.

ALL IN THE SAME MOMENT

Buddha fountain bubbles
Prayer wheel rings
Heater booms on
Power saw buzzes
Meditation legs ache
All in the same moment

MT. MADONNA REDWOODS

I

Nine young redwoods
circling remains
of mother tree,
her body charred
wishbone
ten-feet high.

Children born
from maternal ashes
like a flock
of arboreal phoenixes.

II

Redwood stump
like green mountain
stream,
mosses cascading
down
her terraced contours
flowing, flowing, flowing
onto rocks
below.

From her dead
center
delicate seedling
rises
festooned with
spider webs.

III

Young stub
still attached
to mother
trunk
grows tender
bark over
severed end
like torn limb
sprouting
new flesh
where blood
once flowed.

IV

Through core
of massive log
lodged
at waterfall lip
the stream flows,
her cold mountain
waters seeming
to rejuvenate
old veins.

V

O rotting log
at side
of trail,
how good
to see you
again

after losing
my way
and finding
it and you
once more.

SWEETGUM IN SUMMER LIGHT

Like a great green diamond
atop a tall granite pedestal
you flashed your life so exuberantly.

And I, a passerby, suddenly felt
heart clench and eyes tear.

Walking on I wondered: was it awe
alone that so shattered me?

Or was there also a touch
of envy?

SQUIRREL SCIENCE

Miming the squeaks of squirrel
seems to stir his curiosity
and turn him into scientist.

He experiments with sound,
suddenly stopping or starting,
testing or investigating,
if I'll continue aping him—
I do.

At length he grows silent,
perhaps tired of inquiry
or certain of knowledge
or satisfied he's in control.

VOICE OF THE WOODS

Just days before
millennial turn
I sit cross-legged
on rickety planks
suspended
by young redwoods
high above Land
of Medicine Buddha
witnessing
in joy and peace
the surrounding trees, birds, bugs,
sky, flickering sunlight
in timeless
repose
. . .
then hear
Voice of the Woods
and am filled
with quiet
excitement.

It feels like a sacred
calling:
these marvelous creatures
beckoning me
to speak on their behalf.

How precious
and undefended
they are!

How imperiled
are all
without human
words!

Daily they speak
to us
in their own
eloquent ways
yet we do not hear
or wish to know
what they're saying.

What a great responsibility,
what a grave and urgent duty,
to voice their beauty,
their wisdom, their right
to be!

Surely they're pleading,
Cherish us! Protect us!
We are your relations!

SITRA ACHRA*

The Name

of God

super-

imposed

on smoke-

stacks of

Auschwitz

*In Jewish mysticism, Sitra Achra refers to the "Other Side" of God; it is the aspect of divinity that gives rise to evil, chaos and destruction. Evil forces, sometimes personified as demons, may emerge in the spiritual and material realms when divine judgment and anger become extreme or when other divine energies become excessive or out of balance. Frequently, these excesses and imbalances are caused by human vice according to the principle "as below, so above," but sometimes they occur within the Godhead for mysterious reasons that have nothing to do with human iniquity.

OCEAN OF DARKNESS

O vast still silent ocean
of darkness
surrounding and centering
each wave point
of energy

O deep deep silence
suffusing
every sweetsuffering
song

O imageless wellspring
imagining
every shape
and shadow

O timeless womb
conceiving
eon
upon
eon

O point within point
within point
projecting world
after world
after world

THE HARMONY OF HEAVENLY BODIES

All night our sleeping bodies
press together
fuse rib to rib
refuse the cold
lonely spaces
between stars
squeeze gentle heat
from slumbering passion

All night feeling your touch
and your turns
an arm lingering
on my chest
warm breath caressing
ear and neck
a foot that slides
slowly down my leg
til it finds
a foot
and rests there
content
toes entwining toes

All night your wondrous
image
shimmers in dreams
like a full moon
in summer sky
til suddenly
my eyes open wide
craving sight of you
and see your eyes

spring open too
dark almonds
silvered with flames
and in that moment
as if by request
the radio plays
your favorite song
Ode to Joy!

EARLY SPRING ON MT. TAM

Young redwood twisted
open
by El Nino winds and rains

Huge moist slit rosy
like lover's lips

Old stump gleams wet redbrown
in spring sun

Chunks of rotting wood flake
like grilled salmon flesh

Oaks everywhere bedecked
in multigreen mosses

Terraced rock wall
so mossed over seems
a vernal waterfall

Two snails a handbreadth apart
bulge out of madrone bark
like dark staring eyes

WATER SPIDERS

Water spiders like jet-
propelled crosses
flash across
surface
of pond
dedicated
to Awakened One.*

*The Awakened One is Gautama Buddha.

BLUEBIRD COUPLE

Through the whirring

dance of flies

I see

a bluebird couple

playing

in the light

filled

limbs of an oak

DIPPING INTO DARKNESS

Dipping
into darkness
we lift
black waters
of life
into light

Turning
away from sun
we see
our shadows
in lightened
relief

SILENT BELL

My breath
a silent bell
always ringing
always awakening
me to what is and is not
right here
right
now

FORBIDDEN FOODS:
Childhood Memories of Paradise by the Lake

I. Breakfast

The stove smokes and sizzles like an altar
as Aunt Fran, aproned in white and yellow,
ministers to eight thick strips of bacon
that wiggle, palpitate and pop, their meat
tanning dark red, their fat translucent gold.

When color and crunch reach perfection,
her spatula swoops down and scoops up
the glistening slices whose amber beads,
alive with heat, drip drip drip into the pan
and hop and sputter in diminishing arcs.

Near the stove, layers of paper towels
curl up like sheets torn from holy scrolls.
On these she places the strips in rows,
covers them over with several more layers
and pats them gently with her wrinkled hands.

As she sets new slices on the skillet,
I lift the covers, pilfer two fat fellows
and gobble them down guiltily, savoring
the essence of their forbidden flavors.

She winks and smiles at me—but Mom barks,
"Wait til breakfast!" and Dad, aroused, looks up
from his newspaper and stares vaguely
at me, like a rabbi interrupted
during Talmud study. He sighs and then
returns to reading. In Michiana Shores

he accepts Aunt Fran's indulgent rule
and for a month grants us pagan pleasures.

II. Lunch

Towels dangle from necks, and beach chairs
loop over shoulders, as we hurry home
from the lake, silently contemplating
what surprise Aunt Fran will serve for lunch.
Yesterday's treat was hot corned beef that Ted,
the butcher, trimmed extra lean. Ted smokes fat
cigars and talks out the other side of
his mouth and wears big white aprons blotched with
every shape and shade of blood and mom says
he cheats on poor Jean, his short plump wife who runs
the register sitting on her wood stool.

We linger in the yard for the big tan
Cadillac to return and run to meet
it parking beside our Chevy wagon.
The window hums down, and we hear, "Hi boys!"
and reply, "Hi Aunt Fran!" The door locks click
open and Aunt Fran bustles out, toting
her big beige purse with the golden clasp.

In the cavernous trunk stand three full bags
carefully placed by Johnnie, Ted's six foot
three son who, Cousin Babe says, is turning
into a lady's man just like his dad.
I grab a bag brimming with packages,
and my brothers do the same and follow
me along the sidewalk, up the green steps,
through the long living room, to the kitchen
table, where we plunk down our heavy loads.

Unwrapping the crisp white parcels feels like
opening birthday presents or Christmas
gifts (though we've never celebrated
that day). Inside is a World Series
roster of meats: ten thick sirloin steaks, one
massive tenderloin roast, four whole chickens,
a dozen slabs of babyback pork ribs,
and two colossal kosher salamis.

Bob and Al watch as I reach in and pull
out the last white package. "It's hot," I say,
feeling the heat through the paper. "It's hot,"
says Bob, rubbing his hands together. "Hot,"
says Al, his face brightening to a red ball.
I break the seal and unfold the paper.
"It's ham," I shout, and they applaud wildly
as if I'd introduced the Beatles.

Aunt Fran looks on, beaming and blushing.

REDWOOD BIRD

A bird
flies up
from one branch
to another
quickly searching
needles for insects.

Why don't you begin
at the top
and just float
down
from branch
to branch?

Because I
enjoy
asserting
my strength.

TREE BODY

Looking up
in empty
moment
I suddenly
slide
between seconds
and see
a self-
vision
just above:
braided branches burst
out shoulders
wild webbed roots flash
down through feet
massive trunk explodes
torso and splits shirt
shimmering green crown hovers
high over head.

WALKING

Walking tall
shoulders back
chest out
stomach in
teeth clenched
I slice through air
my head a giant eye
swiveling to and fro
atop a moving pillar
like a portable
panopticon
surveying
its domain.

Then suddenly I remember
myself and bend knees slightly and let
arms drop naturally while loosening jaw
and breathing in and out through soft belly center
and instantly the world becomes widerrounderfuller
and seems to grow out of me like a glimmering
pulsing four dimensional web
spun from vital core

THRICE BORN:
for Cind

Why have you left us–still so young and full
of dreams? Still so wet with living waters
of second birth. Your soft strong wings just
beginning to unfold as you bravely
shed five decades of self-doubt and reproach
and reached deep deep into your beautiful soul
and found there rivers of astonishing love
and loveliness that touched and held the heart.

On my desk still sit your two meditation
cards with their elegant, Zen-like
reminders of Silence and Celebration.
Yet today they bring me as much grief
as guidance. Today they seem to remind
me to quietly experience your sudden
passing and find some way—perhaps this way—
to celebrate your passage to other realms.

On my poetry shelf stands the luminous
little book you crafted with gracious
fingers and filled with wise and holy words
and swirls of rainbow hues afloat in black
circles and crescents and a few torn scraps.

Could it be you dove so deeply into
your Creative Source and found there such bliss
and peace that She decided to keep you
with Her always—to be Her soul mate day
and night? . . . . Yes, I can see you bathing
and frolicking in Her ever shining
fountain of light. This must be your third
and final birth!–into the realm of
eternal splendor you so loved and longed for.

LITERARY TAIL

A poem is a literary tail
of a meteoric moment
of passion or peace,
tracing and intensifying
the subtle karmic ripples
of human experience,
preserving the possibility
and provoking the probability
of like but new encounters.

TURKISH FIGS

When she opens her eyes and sees my gift
of figs—Turkish figs dusted with sugar—
she bursts into spritely peals of laughter,
eyes wrinkling. Into the bag she inserts
two slender fingers and snatches the plumpest
fruit by its hard stubby tail and twirls it
back and forth, back and forth, until a thought
swells her eyes. Then her long crimson nails press
into the sun-shriveled flesh and tear the sac
in two. Offering me half, she pushes her thumbs
into back of other half and inverts it
to gilded demidome specked with seeds.
The golden light dances on her pupils,
and she kneads the pulp until her finger tips
gleam too. And with a wink, she balances
the manipulated morsel on her tongue,
which, like a pink cobra, weaves in the air
before retracting into its moist warm home,
then leaps out to lick my sticky lips.

MY CAT'S ADVICE ON JOB HUNTING

Get up at dawn—it's a new day.
Feel the sun on your face,
stretch, breathe deeply, shake
yourself awake. Eat a good
breakfast high in protein. Drink
some water. Go outside for some
fresh air. Take a little relaxed
walk and notice the way the trees
look, the plants smell, the wind
sounds. Above all, enjoy

yourself. Remember each moment
is an adventure. Always
keep your eyes open—the world
ever sends you signals. Listen
to the sounds, the voices,
the vibrations. Feel them
along the length of your body.
Flee the dangerous presences,
investigate the inviting ones.

If something seems really
appealing, check it out
some more: smell it, walk around
it, touch it, give it a little
lick. Stay with it as long
as there is something alive
and enlivening. When you sense
the attraction waning,
move on. Do what you like.
Repeat what you love.

Insist on having what really
feeds you, body and soul.

Whine and persist in whining
until you get it. Be willing
to eat what is offered but
keep asking for what you really
desire. You need to let others
know you're serious and determined
to get what you want. But

you have to be sure you really
want it. Don't think too much.
Stop making those crazy lists
of pros and cons. Use your senses,
your instincts, your intuitions.
Let your head follow your belly
and heart. Keep yourself clean
and well groomed. Make sure
you get your head and back rubbed
at least once a day by someone

you love and trust. When you find
the job you really want, stalk it,
observe it quietly, study
its movements and patterns
and then pounce before it gets
away. Pounce, and if you miss,
pounce again, and if it gets away,
then seek a fresh opportunity,

forgetting the disappointment
of failure but remembering
the approaches that helped
and those that didn't. Keep honing
your hunting strategies—the better
they become, the better the job
you'll land. The more skilled
the cat, the juicier the catch!

THE TREE THAT TREMBLED ME

Earth and rain course
through my roots
and up my trunk
like torrents of rising
light rushing rushing
rushing through my girth
spilling out my bark
spreading up to branches
like lightning
shattering upward
sparking outward
into leafy fireworks
that green the sky
and fall back to earth
in shimmering showers

PELICAN PARADISE

I

Unmoving mounds
of foam
on wavy lagoon
are five
white pelicans
huddled happily.

II

Along the ridge of giant ocean wave
a brown pelican surfs sideways
just above the breaking
frothing
crest.

SCREAMING SEA

Sunk
in silent
depths
of nature
meditation
devoted
to well-being
of all beings
I suddenly
hear
the heart-
crucifying
cries
of sea
creatures
screaming
in agony
from all
the toxins
and trash
desecrating
the Earth—
a chorus
of anguish
so urgent
I feel I
must
do something
anything
soon

ADAM

Once Adam
was all
all alone
was one
and wanted
no one.

Then Adam
saw two
felt lone-
some
and wanted
one too
felt less
than one
without
a two.

So Adam
became
Adam-Eve
two-in-one
living in one
great bliss
till too different
wants split them
into two fierce
duelers.

Now Adam and Eve
want their wants
united in one loving
harmony.

COLOSSAL CANOPY

How wondrous
to see colossal canopy
of hundred foot redwood
swaying in summer breeze
like great green
flower!
Or
was it
a mass of moss
floating in sea blue sky
and sending forth thick brown
frond into receptive
earth below?

RISING LOTUS

Midstream in meditation
my thoughts suddenly center
on you
and I feel my lotus
starting
to
r
i
s
e
!

ASCENDING ARCS

shingled bark
of soquel
redwood fes-
tooned with
ascending
arcs of spider
webs that catch
golden needles
but no bugs

SANDHILL

Between the lake and Aunt Fran's house stands
the sandhill, rising above the tallest oaks
and embroidered with jade and emerald vines.
In early morning I begin my expedition up
the slope along the broad path that snakes
among the filigree of leaves and stems
and roots. Hunched over I climb like a chimp:
arms swing to and fro as toes sift the sand.
I rise and sink, rise and sink, while gold
cascades fall and flow beneath me. Squirrels
on every side track my progress with furry
periscopes, and jays perched above me
laugh and whistle at my slow ascent.

Panting I arrive at the hill's bald crown
and scan the surface for yesterday's prints:
a swirl of feet, a blurred body, more feet,
another body with fans for limbs. Inspired,
I slump down and roll around and around
squirming like some prehistoric creature
I read about in Dr. Zim's dinosaur book.
Breathless I lie on my back and listen
to my heart gallop, then canter, then trot.
Uncounted minutes drift with the clouds;
the sun warms my throat; the sand cools my nape.
Up again I race to the meadow's edge where,
belly down, I search the seam between lake and sky
for traces of the city we leave each August:
tiny gray silhouettes waver in the distance.
Nearer in a lone swimmer glides beyond
the bobbing red posts. He floats and plays
like a sea lion, then swims back to shore.

Down the winding trail I dash, swerving right
and left, right and left, flying over roots,
tilting into the sand, churning up a zigzagging
storm that dogs me down the hill. As bottom
nears I leap forward, tumble down, tumble over
and over and over again in wild motion,
more motion, hilarious motion. Then stop.
And breathe again. Unroll. And watch the hill spin
around and round as in Disney movies.

SHIVA

I

I dance on bones
of illusion
overbrimming
the world

Where my feet fall
gluttonous jaws crack
haughty necks shatter
mean ribs splinter
rank shanks pulverize

All dissolve and return
to bubbling cauldron
where new world brews
stirred by stern-eyed chef
who too dissolves at dawn

II

Whirling whirling whirling
my pith bleeds outward
in widening spires
till surfaces flush clear
and perimeters perish
and all permeates all

III

Leaping from skull to skull
like a child
hopping from stone to stone
I am at one
with life and death

TREE AT EDGE OF CAMPUS

I

Young tree planted
near admin building
seems to grow freely
in full spring light.

II

Trunk balanced
perfectly
yet no two branches
make perfect
symmetry.

III

A stone's throw away
beyond barbed fence
wooded hills commence.

LEAVES

exfol-
iation
l e a v e s o u t
trunc-
ation
leave-
s
in

MY CHILDREN

Walking these hills alone,
the sun a blinding white eye,
I see my precious children
and feel myself the father
I might have been.

My eldest son,
New Year's surprise
over eight years ago,
lanky and timid as a reed,
eyes keen and curious
as his mother's dark orbs,
clings to my left hand
to brace his frame
against the golden shock
of daffodils
trumpeting spring.

My soft round daughter,
St. Valentine's gift
just six winters ago,
big-hearted like her mother
and sporting eyes blue as ice;
she swings my right hand,
points with hers and asks
can she pet the pretty dog
coming toward us.

My wet-cheeked baby boy,
conceived in spasms
of thoughtless bliss
two summers ago,

sleeps on my back
like a papoose
and dreams of next summer
when he can run ahead,
more wild and free
than his mother.

But as I near home
my unborn children vanish
and their mothers disappear
and I shudder at our sins
of aborted dreams
and cruel convenience.

THREE

I love the joiners and binders
and linkers of things
I love the connectors the communers
the lovers of beings
I love the mediators the arbitrators
the messengers of possibility
the weavers of cloth tapestry and tale
the uniters the healers the builders of peace

Those who give and those who serve
Those who see and those who conceive
Those who dream and those who dare
Those who hear and those who care
I kiss caress cherish them all

With silence I surround
With stillness I encompass
With hands hearts and loins I embrace
With mucus semen and sweat I seal

With fire I weld
and with water I meld
With air I ring
and with earth I ground

Rifts I knit and frays I mend
Hurts I soothe and wounds I salve

I reconcile conflicts
and resolve contradictions
I companion oppositions
and befriend paradoxes

In between this and that
now and then
here and there
in and out
above and below
swirls swells sluices my love

I circulate among centers of being
and concentrate in circles of life
I commute between realms
and translate one to another

I am the transformation and the transfiguration
transmuting caterpillar to butterfly
I am the transition and the transportation
ferrying back and ferrying forth

Through communication I spread
Through conjugation I increase
Through confrontation I evolve
Through polarity I equipoise

Yin and yang I yoke
Warp and woof I wed
Stamen and pistol I marry
High and low I betrothe

I am the third thing that begets
and the triple being that births
I am the divine presence that consoles
and the holy spirit that inspires

From duos I burst
and from pairs I bound
From doubles I branch
and from binaries I bud

Wellspring and offspring
Parent and child am I

In rhythm of rain
and cadence of cloud
in tempo of wind
and cycling of sun
is my dance of creation

With heap pile stack I collect
With collage pastiche assemblage I cohere
With pattern process system I compose

In the feast of existence
I am the chef the pot the fire
I am the ingredients the recipes the meal
I am the bliss inside each bite

SHADES OF GREEN

In one small patch

of redwood for-

est I see more

shades of green than

I can name—or

that can be named!

Ah! Infinite

viriditas!

SWEETGUM IN WINTER LIGHT

Young

pear-shaped

sweetgum dropping

deep pink and yellow flames

on grass and sidewalk while nearby

older tree still clings to last green embers,

its base lightly speckled with shades of salmon

and safron, its crown orange and rust-red like

harvest time. . . . I realize so much of the delight

I take in these trees is the bliss of the Infinite

appreciating its own

creation.

THE TREES OF LIFE ARE FALLING

My prayer walk
      through the park
Is assailed
      this morning
By grizzly
      grinding sounds
Of chain saws
      buzzing, buzzing,
Buzzing through
      hearts
Of eucalyptus,
      the latest
      victims
Of human
      progress.

In the name
      of electric
      force,
For the sake
      of modern
      civilization,
Tall trees
      are being razed
      to the ground
For they grow
      too near
      the lines
      of power.

Holy, holy, holy
      is the Lord
      of Hosts.

Heavy, heavy, heavy
        is my heart
        of flesh.
Killing, killing, killing
        are the machines
        of men.

The trees of life
        are falling
The trees of life
        are falling

So we can indulge
        our comforts
And fill
        our pockets
And consume
        the Earth.

Even though I walk
        through the valley
Of the shadow
        of death
I will fear
        no evil
For You are
        with me.

Yet the cogs
        of commerce
        continue to turn,
And the chips
        of technology
        hum faster and faster
        out of control,

And the engines
     of greed grow
     more and more
     insatiable.

The trees of life
     are falling
The trees of life
     are falling

When will we cease
     to eat
From the Tree of Power
     and Progress?

OYSTER

Cold and chaotic currents purl
and jostle her this way and that,
dash her fluted workshop
against the sea's scalloped floor,
rocking the sphere of her secret labor.

Yet within her wondrous lab,
she silently perseveres
in expressing her liquid loveliness,
translucent as blood soaked in sun,
and layer by layer, year by year,
transforms the once irritating atom
of rough rock, dust of sea,
waste of ages, into startling
globe of enameled light,
the sea's own brilliant moon.

MY BEST BOOK OF POEMS

My best book of poems
never passed through hands
yet composed they were
one miraculous morn
in bright summer air
by creatures I met
on slow meandering walk
up neighboring hill.

Simple exquisite words
tongued by flowers, trees,
rocks, curbs and cars
revealing rare insight
and eloquence—
each poem unique
and concentrated
like a dazzling haiku.

Thrice I asked myself
should I record these gems
for future inspiration
or would pen and pad
stifle their freeflowing
genius. . . . I chose
to listen and marvel
in amazement.

Yet the very next day
I regretted my decision
and strained in vain
to recall the precious
voices.

Again and again
I visited them
but they were silent—
their wisdom lost
forever
to the winds . . .

O, how I longed
to be or become
a reader of breezes!

FAMILY PORTRAITS OF THE FUTURE

In family

portraits of the future

wild doves are perched

on shoulders

of mothers, fathers, daughters and sons

gathered round

trees of life

rooted deep

in rich dark

Earth

I AM

In the beginnings
I am
And in the endings
I am
Every finish but a pause
Every start but a push
Or pull
Of infinite pulsations
Of endless cyclings and recyclings
Birthings and buryings
Bloomings and bustings

All I see is I
I is all I see
All always all
Always each
Always all

Each a part a portal
A prism

Enter a leaf
You are there
Enter a root
You are here
Branch trunk fruit
Tree of life

Earth is Sun's
Dark condensed
Rays
Sun is Earth's

Light loosened
Dust

Waves dissolve
Into particles
Particles dance
Into waves

Can you see an apple
Without seeing the branch
The sun the dirt the ants
The spring rain the clouds
The nearby lake the distant sea
The farmer the trucker the steel plant
The rubber plantation
The marketplace

I am the mother and the baby
And the flow of joy between
I am the mammaries and the milk
And the mouth that sucks blind

The trees are my thick hairs
The mountains muscled bone
The seas fragrant sweat
The winds living breath

I split myself to see myself
To know my nature
To gaze upon my face
To proclaim my facets

With division I multiply
With difference I make sense

One to act
Another to react
One to be
Another to become
One to know
Another to be known

I make worlds out of yearning
For partners
In dance

Worlds whirl out
And worlds whirl in
But never do I release
Both hands

Lovewrestling is the combat
I love most

I rip my stillness
To make delirious dance
And score my quietude
To make uproarious song

Chaos is my free play
Order my moment of rest

I splinter my eye
To make points of view
I gather my eyes
To know myself
Completely

I burn and burn
Consuming myself
Spreading out my wealth
That all may be
Light

Everyone
A ray
Rooted
In my burning
Heart

Everyone
A root
Arrayed
With my fire

My heart a bright home
An incandescent loam

Elemental Wisdom

EARTH WISDOM

Be porous
enough
to receive
life-giving
rains

～

Be sturdy
enough
to bear
weight
of many
beings

～

Darkness abounds
for billions
burrowed below

～

Enrich yourself
by lying fallow
for a season

～

Even mighty beings
begin as tiny seeds

To raise your reach,
deepen your roots

~

Darkness longs
to flower
lightward

~

The living feast
on the deceased

~

Lotus raises loving ladder
linking mud, pond and sky

~

From muddled muck
green glory grows

~

Dying bodies
build
living beauties

Green springs
from kiss
of sun
and shade

~

Soft soil
outlives
rough rock

~

Molten magma gleams
beneath cool dim stone

~

Earthbound
birth
airborne

~

Darkness loves to dress
in peacock plumes

~

Night longs for day
and day for darkness

Light dyes darkness
living emerald

~

We're spun
by the Spinner
of universes

~

Our bodies harbor
pools, ponds and oceans
of emotions

~

Sink still foundations
to shoulder your motions

~

Journey inward
to your hidden
home

~

Beware of prophets
who ask you to forsake
your physical foundations

Even airborne return
to soil and sea

~

As spring light dispels
midwinter gloom,
come forth from your caves,
dens and burrows

~

New mounts of growth
uprise
where plates of self
collide

~

Life and death are mead
of immortality

~

Mud is milk
to lilies

~

Plain soil
launches
great souls

Mulch old habits,
grow fresh deeds

~

Seek the root
of things

~

WATER WISDOM

When struck
by stone or stare,
let pummeling force ripple
outward in widening spires

~

As emotions billow
out of conrol,
remember mellow currents
lumbering below

~

Purity and putridity
are matters
of concentration

~

Extract the pollutant
or
expand the pool

~

Though we take different
routes across the river
we're sure to meet again
on the other side

Better to flow around,
over or under a boulder
than force your way through

~

When you're grave
as dirt-black clouds,
let your tears rain
down and revive
your bonedry soul

~

Steady showers
quicken crops,
sudden deluges
flatten fields,
hellish twisters
harrow grounds

~

Let inner
river
move you
to see

~

To catch spirit
in your sails
you may need
to tack to and fro

A snake streams
side to side
showing the way
of progress

~

A fish knows
the shortest distance
between two points
is a wavy line

~

Far wiser to correct
and recorrect
along the way
than strain to hold
a strait straight course

~

Placid rivers of wisdom
nourish more creatures
than rushing arroyos
of information

~

Your flowing being
shows shifting contours
of terrains you've traveled

As heart frosts with fear,
fluid acts fast freeze

〜

There are rivers upon rivers
running through every limb
and leaf of your life

〜

Dark thoughts, dark words, dark deeds
begrime vital functions

〜

Mind caught and cuffed
by dizzying dazzle
of shattered surfaces

〜

Wait in stillness
till murk settles

〜

Let soul waves
mirror sun rays

Unknown creatures
of magnificence
swim in silence
in your shadowy
depths

∼

When aboil,
keep your lid
slightly ajar

∼

Impediments give
rippling beauty
to life currents

∼

Beware of running too long
or too hard
uphill

∼

Tend the roots
of your friends;
leaves will grow
on their own

Flash floods of deeds
engulf the ground
you hurry on

~

Evaporate to rise,
condense to fall

~

Gain Neptunian force
by sinking
to soul's dark floor

~

When feelings chill like sleet
you're sure to slip

~

Rains of compassion
douse conflagrations
of hatred and greed

~

The chill of terror
reveals life's crystalline cast
and future casket

A drop of warm feeling
melts mounds of snowflakes

~

Stagnant feelings putrify

~

Suss out root route,
follow stem street,
flow through leafy lanes

~

A cup of poison intention
can pollute life's pure lake

~

No fluidity, no vitality

~

As you heat up
you'll feel pressured
to express yourself

~

Let soul fish eat
ego plankton

Mist masks
the light
of mystery

～

Whether emotions assume
liquid, solid or gaseous form
depends on your temperature

～

As mind fog
burns away,
soul alights
like midday

～

Leave life's shore
to plumb soul
deep currents

～

Keep moving to stay
fresh and effervescent

～

Though new water
continually arrives
the whirl of the pool
maintains its mold

Surges of feeling
can soak or sink
an unmoored soul

~

Crosscurrents
give way
to serene seas

~

Start your day
with a chalice
of morning dew

~

The bubble of your being
was born in infinite sea—
and will return there.

~

AIR WISDOM

All life glides
by grace

~

We float
in invincible
oceans of air

~

Emptiness is full
of ethereal force

~

The invisible connects
as well as cleaves

~

The odor of a thing
reveals its relative
rot or robustness

~

Unseen currents
bend trees
and boil oceans

A sudden breeze
can sweep your life

～

Calm clarity resides
at the center
of spiraling violence—
return there!

～

Let mind wax sky-vast
and wane sky-empty
while watching thought-clouds
and mist-moods glide by

～

A storm is ever
circling somewhere—
await your turn!

～

Twisting uproots

～

Bee-wing winds in Boston
stir storms in Bombay

Ethereal porters
carry
living waters

~

Know the invisible
by its vibrations
in the veils of life

~

Dark space paves
light's highway

~

The nectar of ether
is ever nourishing you

~

Be a spruce
supplely swaying
to spirit's
undulations

~

For freshness
seek the heights

The void is busily
creating the ark
of existence

~

The clearer the medium,
the more transparent
the message

~

Spirit breezes
tickle heart leaves

~

The expiration of redwoods
is the inspiration of bluebirds

~

We're all joined
by flux and interflux
of felt fields of force

~

The space between us
is the clasp that binds us

~

Intangible winds
are touching you

Aura is spirit
made manifest

~

Ether's motions
moan through hormones
of sad and mad

~

Love is stirred by scent
of another's essence.

~

A chance fragrance
can alter your destiny

~

Spores of splendor
are winging their way
to you—prepare the soil
of your soul

~

Let heart hear
harmonies
of hidden stars

How do you know if
you're peopling empty air
with mystifying fancies
or decoding soul-crowded winds
with mystic imaginings?

~

What suffocates the owl
resuscitates the oak

~

Our life transpires
from breath to breath

~

Rhythms of ether
entrain cadences
of earth, water and fire

~

A sudden gust
can snap centuries
of gorgeous growth

~

Build sway
into your structures
or you'll weep more
than willows

Open your pores
wide to imbibe
while not losing
what's inside

~

High and mighty pressures
rush to low and humble places

~

The color of sky
is not the color of sky—
reflect on that!

~

The pause between
in-breath
and out-breath
is the vital turn
in life's unceasing
circuit

~

The void is dyed
living colors
by beings it engulfs

On days of heart-
shattering beauty
spirits shudder
behind the scenes

~

Swirling forces
suck out your life

~

Atmosphere grounds
Earth's figure

~

Life winds waft
through each cell
of your self

~

Breathe in spirit,
breathe out ego

~

Such much depends
on unseen graces

~

FIRE WISDOM

Keep dancing,
let no two moves
flame alike

~

Grow transparent
at your apex

~

You burn only as bright
as your fuel allows

~

If soul becomes soggy
its light is lost in mist

~

Transmute the touchable
into the transparent

~

Wind incandesces,
wet douses,
the soul

Flames of fervor
transfigure
quarks into galaxies,
stars into subatomic ash

~

We're all sun's children
conceived in fiery womb
suckling blazing breasts
bathed in flames of love

~

Body bliss
is bonfire

~

Melting melds,
soaking unseams

~

Hot matters rise,
rising matters cool,
cooling matters sink

Fire whips winds
boils seas
anneals earth
yet can be blown out,
doused and buried
by its elemental kin

~

Dawn sun ignites
earthly ardor—
hear sparrow sing!

~

A spark of spirit
can raze
a forest of difficulties

~

When soul catches fire,
no one knows what will be
created or incinerated

~

A great fire
may torch the forest
of your life
releasing buried seeds
of blessing

The lightning of insight
charges
the thunder of deed

~

Whether life bakes or burns
is a matter of degrees

~

A bolt sparked life
in seasoil broth
stirred by wild winds

~

Fire steers elemental cycles
moving water from heaven
to earth and back again
raising and lowering breezes

~

A bonfire
uplifts its fuel

~

The initiating spark
kindles the fate of the act

Let mind sit
like blue blaze
on body wick

~

Rainbow tints stir
in spirit's white light

~

The hue of mood
reveals
the heat of soul

~

Too much or too little
heat
hardens the heart

~

Let spirit cook all
life's ingredients
into flavorful feast

~

Rage incinerates
the world it aims
to secure

Incendiary words
torch the filaments
linking friends

~

The phoenix soars
from its cinders

~

From buried embers
of seed
arise flaunting flames
of rose

~

Plants eat solar fire,
we eat fire eaters

~

Taste the light
in each bite

~

In brown earth
nestle green flares
that only spring
winds and rains
can unfurl

The night sky is astir
with lightyears' old tales
of long forgotten fires

~

The universe is
the multi-tongued flame
of a single silent
spark

~

ABOUT THE POET

CHARLES MICHAEL BURACK is an award-winning poet, writer, teacher, and scholar as well as a creativity coach and spiritual counselor. He is author of *Songs to My Beloved* (Sacred Arts) and *D. H. Lawrence's Language of Sacred Experience* (Palgrave-Macmillan), and his poems, stories, and essays have been published in magazines and journals around the world. His honors include first prize in the international Songs of the Soul Poetry Contest, and the New Scholar Award of the D. H. Lawrence Society of North America. Common Ground honored his series of articles on interfaith and integral spirituality. He is completing a collection of poems, prayers, and meditations inspired by the Kabbalistic Tree of Life, as well as a spiritual autobiography about his multireligious journey. An award-winning professor at John F. Kennedy University, Burack specializes in integrative approaches to psychology, spirituality, and the creative arts. He lives with his wife, Mary Ann Konarzewski, in the San Francisco Bay Area and can be reached at www.charlesburack.com.

www.ingramcontent.com/pod-product-compliance
Lightning Source LLC
LaVergne TN
LVHW041301080426
835510LV00009B/830